BRISBANE

Brisbane, Queensland's State capital, is a riverside city. Broad reaches of the meandering Brisbane River reflect a friendly, cosmopolitan city that makes the most of its subtropical climate. Alfresco dining, riverside promenades, leafy suburbs and shady verandahs are all part of the city's relaxed style.

From its inauspicious beginnings in 1824 as a British penal outpost, Brisbane has metamorphosed into Australia's third largest city. It is a thriving commercial and administrative centre with links through Asia and the Pacific Rim.

With a population nearing two million, Brisbane spreads along a coastal plain and is bound by the shallow waters of Moreton Bay and the forested slopes of the D'Aguilar Range. Residents enjoy the benefits of Brisbane's waterways and parklands throughout its mild winters and sultry summers.

The compact city centre, tucked in a loop of the river, is an intriguing mix of old and new. Modern steel and glass buildings tower over elegant colonial structures of stone and timber. A resurgence in inner city living now brings life and colour to the central business district 24 hours a day.

Beyond the city's urban pleasures lies a wealth of natural attractions. Many small islands and a maze of waterways shelter behind the barrier of Moreton Bay's massive sand islands. To the north and south the sweeping surf beaches of the Gold and Sunshine Coasts give way to hinterland valleys, forests, volcanic escarpments and rich farmlands.

Brisbane is the Sunshine State's most livable city and an ideal gateway to some of Australia's premier tourist destinations.

Steve Parish™
PUBLISHING

Above: *Brisbane city seen across the Town Reach of the Brisbane River.*

BRISBANE: QUEENSLAND'S CAPITAL

The establishment of a convict outpost in 1824 began Brisbane's 35-year transformation from Yuggera tribal land to capital of the British colony of Queensland. As free settlers took up holdings around Brisbane Town, the more adventurous headed to western pasturelands. By the 1860s Brisbane had become a thriving port for south-east Queensland's wool and wheat industries. Over the next hundred years its fortunes were linked to the cyclical nature of primary production and mining. Economic prosperity has seen Brisbane shake off its country town image to reveal a modern capital city. As technology, commerce and tourism take the city into the twenty-first century, a touch of the tropics ensures Brisbane will retain its unique charm.

Above: *Kangaroo Point and the Story Bridge are in the foreground of this view of Brisbane.*
Below: *(Left) City views across the Botanic Gardens. (Right) Over New Farm Park to Kangaroo Point and the city.*

BRISBANE AND ITS RIVER

During colonial days, tall ships sailed up the Brisbane River carrying cargo and passengers into the heart of the settlement. Today, modern port facilities greet ships at the river mouth and major redevelopments upstream have returned the river to the people of Brisbane. Ferries and pleasure craft ply the river's waters, while fashionable apartments and eateries line its banks. Outdoor entertainment, cool riverside promenades and shady landscaped parks offer endless opportunities for both locals and visitors to enjoy the river's many moods.

Top: *The Shafston Reach of the Brisbane River, with Dockside and the Story Bridge top right and New Farm on the right.*
Above: *(Left) A CityCat passes Dockside. (Right) A much-loved mode of travel — cycling along one of the many bike-ways on the banks of the Brisbane River.*

Above: *The Story Bridge and its lights are emphasised by the fireworks of Riverfire, a highlight of spring's Riverfestival.*
Below: *The southern piers of the Story Bridge stand in Captain Burke Park, the northern ones in Petrie Bight. The bridge joins Kangaroo Point to Fortitude Valley.*

Above: *South Bank Parklands, complete with a lagoon and beach, is a great place to relax and enjoy Brisbane's summer weather.*

SOUTH BANK PARKLANDS

Since hosting World Expo 1988, South Bank has evolved into a 16-hectare oasis where leisure and cultural pursuits mingle against the backdrop of the city's centre. Lush gardens featuring an arbor of bougainvillea set the scene for a relaxing Brisbane experience. South Bank is a great place for a family outing: it has something for everyone. The riverside promenade, palm-fringed lagoon and market stalls attract thousands of visitors on weekends. Outdoor movies, concerts, fireworks displays and a passing parade of sightseers provide year-round entertainment. There are plenty of restaurants and cafés that offer good food and wonderful city views.

Above and clockwise: *The Goodwill Bridge spans the Brisbane River to connect South Bank and the city centre; bougainvillea, a bright addition to many a Brisbane garden, decorates South Bank's Arbour; the flags of many nations fly proudly at South Bank; South Bank Craft Markets; South Bank lagoon is a waterplay area adjoining the river.*

Above: *Kangaroo Point is bounded by (left) the Town Reach and (right) the Shafston Reach of the Brisbane River. It is connected to Fortitude Valley by the Story Bridge.*
Below: *A view of the city centre's high-rise buildings behind the green mangrove-fringed expanse of the City Botanic Gardens.*

Top: *Sculptures decorate the waterfront at the base of the Kangaroo Point cliffs.*
Above: *(Left) A riverside tribute to the rowers who use the river. (Right) Dockside with the Story Bridge in the distance.*

KANGAROO POINT AND DOCKSIDE

Kangaroo Point is one of many pockets of land created by the Brisbane River's looping course. Home owners and apartment dwellers seek out its views of the river and city. Picnic facilities and an award-winning boardwalk run along the base of the cliffs, a favourite rock-climbing venue. The Dockside apartments, restaurants and marina form a bustling complex on the Shafston Reach opposite New Farm.

Above: *Looking across the Brisbane River to Eagle Street Pier and the Riverside Promenade.*
Below: *(Left) Cascades at the Riverside Centre. (Right) Paddlewheelers offer travellers a leisurely trip along the Brisbane River.*

RIVERSIDE

Brisbane's enthusiasm for reclaiming its river has infiltrated the financial end of town. An excellent boardwalk links the area's waterfront attractions, which include the magnificently restored Customs House, built from 1886 and opened in 1889. The Riverside Centre spills past the Brisbane Stock Exchange and flows on to Eagle Street Pier. Both complexes offer eateries that suit all tastes and budgets. A carnival atmosphere prevails on Sunday as visitors and market stalls crowd the riverside terraces. Sightseers can indulge themselves on board old-time paddlewheelers or catch a CityCat ferry for river trips between Hamilton and St Lucia.

Above: *Market stalls delight shoppers at the Eagle Street Pier complex.*

Above: *The Railway Central clock is in the left front of this view across Anzac Square and Post Office Square to the Post Office.*

CITY CENTRE AND FORTITUDE VALLEY

Brisbane's central business district is contained by a small grid of streets named after British royalty of the colonial era. Public squares, arcades and shady street trees make it a user-friendly centre that can be crossed in about 20 minutes. The city's retail hub is Queen Street Mall, where shopping and entertainment are on offer seven days a week.

Fortitude Valley predates Queen Street as Brisbane's retail centre. It was here in the 1860s that local farmers set up a produce market. A fledgling Chinatown soon followed, and has grown into one of the Valley's main attractions. Other drawcards include weekend retro markets and a lively café, music and club scene.

Above: Brisbane's City Hall offers city views from its tower observation deck. It includes an art gallery and museum. King George Square is a popular meeting place.
Below: (Left) Traffic-free Queen Street Mall is the place to shop, dine or go to the cinema. (Right) Markets are held in Fortitude Valley's Brunswick Street Mall each Saturday.

BRISBANE'S PUBLIC GARDENS

Part of Brisbane's reputation as a livable city stems from its public gardens, which provide both respite from city streets and venues for special events. The City Botanic Gardens is a 16-hectare haven of broad lawns, multi-hued flower beds and outstanding specimen trees. Downriver, New Farm Park is well known for its rose gardens and splendid avenue of Jacarandas. An obstacle course within the aerial roots of huge fig trees appeals particularly to children.

The Mt Coot-tha Botanic Gardens, just 8 kilometres from the CBD is a 52-hectare living museum displaying Australian and exotic plants in rainforest, arid, woodland and wetland settings. Among its treasures are a scented garden that excites the senses and a Japanese garden that soothes the spirit.

Above: *New Farm Park, accessible by CityCat, provides green spaces to which Brisbane people gravitate to relax, stroll or picnic.*

Top: *(Left) The charming inner-city garden in E McCormick Place on Roma Street. (Right) The lookout over the "Flying Duck" built into the lake in the Roma Street Parkland.*
Centre: *(Left) Inside the Mt Coot-tha Botanic Gardens geodesic dome that houses tropical plants. (Right) The lake in the Mt Coot-tha Botanic Gardens, a sanctuary for waterfowl.*
Below: *(Left) Brisbane's City Botanic Gardens, established in 1855. (Right) The boardwalk giving access to the river and mangroves that border the City Botanic Gardens.*

Above: *The view of Brisbane city from the lookout on Mt Coot-tha.*

Below: *(Left) Terraces on Mt Coot-tha give access to wonderful views of Brisbane and its environs. (Right) Telescopes sharpen the view from Mt Coot-tha Lookout.*

MT COOT-THA AND BRISBANE FOREST PARK

A scenic drive winds up Mt Coot-tha to reveal a remarkable panorama. The view sweeps around from the peaks of the Border Range, across the city to Moreton Bay and northward to the Glass House Mountains. Brisbane Forest Park stretches north and west along the D'Aguilar Range, encompassing eucalypt forest, woodland and subtropical rainforest. Within the park, national parks, state forest and council reserves provide a range of outdoor recreation facilities.

Above: *The Summit Restaurant and Kuta Café are sited at Mt Coot-tha Lookout.*
Below: *(Left and right) Rainforest on Mt Glorious, in Maiala National Park, a section of Brisbane Forest Park.*

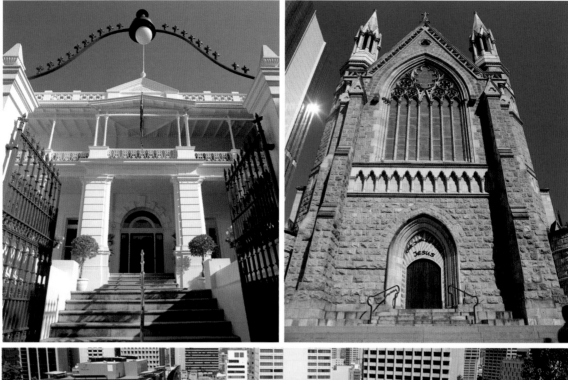

Top: *(Left) The Queensland Club in Alice Street, opposite the City Botanic Gardens, was finished in 1884. (Right) The nave of St Stephen's Cathedral opened in 1874, replacing the chapel that still stands beside it, as Brisbane's main Catholic place of worship.*
Above: *The Old Mill was built by convicts in 1828 to grind maize. It later became a signal post and meteorological observatory.*

HISTORIC BRISBANE

Brisbane takes pride in its architectural heritage. Numerous self-guiding walks through the inner city bring to life the story of Brisbane's evolution. Among places worthy of note, other than those pictured, are the Shrine of Remembrance, Naldham House and the Port Office, all fine examples of Classic Revival style. The Georgian simplicity of the convict-built Commissariat Stores on William Street (the lower floors were built in 1829, the top storey was added in 1913) contrasts with the French Renaissance facade of nearby Parliament House, first used for sittings in 1868.

Above: *The historic Customs House has been restored by the University of Queensland and contains a brasserie, art gallery and bookshop.*
Below: *(Left) The Mansions are at the City Botanic Gardens end of George Street. (Right) Built in 1846, Newstead House is Brisbane's oldest surviving homestead.*

Mainstream and alternative cultural venues abound in Brisbane. The Brisbane Powerhouse on the river at New Farm was added to the scene in 2000. The renovated power station and its surrounds provide wonderful performance spaces for innovative programs of contemporary live arts. At the Queensland Cultural Centre in South Brisbane, visitors can browse through the exhibitions and permanent collections of the State's art gallery, museum and library. This splendid centre is also home to the concert hall and theatres of the Performing Arts Complex. Nearby is the Brisbane Convention and Exhibition Centre, which holds more than 400 events each year.

Above: South Bank is the home of Brisbane's arts scene. The Queensland Performing Arts Centre (or QPAC) showcases a sophisticated selection of local and international plays, operas, musicals, concerts, ballets and other performances.

Top left and clockwise: *State Library of Queensland; the Brisbane Powerhouse Centre for the Live Arts; Gallery of Modern Art;* Flood Sculpture, *by Richard Tipping, at the Powerhouse;* Approaching Equilibrium, *by Anthony Pryor, stands near the Queensland Art Gallery.*

Top: *(Left) South Bank Parklands. (Right) The Regatta Hotel, Coronation Drive, is a well-loved meeting place.*
Above: *Siggi's at the Port Office, Stamford Plaza Brisbane, on Edward Street.*

OUT AND ABOUT IN BRISBANE

Socialising over a good meal or a cool drink is a Brisbane institution. Eateries are plentiful in the city centre and inner suburbs, and range from fine dining establishments to casual coffee bars. For much of the year alfresco is the favoured mode, whether in garden courtyards or at streetside tables. A cosmopolitan population gives the city a world of cuisines, each making the most of local produce, fresh seafood and seasonal tropical fruits.

Paddington, West End, Milton and Fortitude Valley are well-patronised dining precincts that offer a choice of food styles. There are many riverfront restaurants with the added bonus of magnificent city views. Brisbane pubs, many dating back to the 1800s, are the city's original purveyors of hospitality and continue to be popular meeting places.

Above: *Park Road, Milton, is lined with places to meet, eat and enjoy.*
Below: *The Ann Street entrance to the Chinatown Mall in the Valley.*

Above: *A Statue of Sir Thomas Ryan, Queensland Premier 1915–19, stands in Queens Gardens, in front of the Conrad International Brisbane Hotel.*
Below: *(Left) A statue of Queen Victoria, and (right) the Wedge-tailed Eagle, emblem of the Royal Australian Air Force, in Queens Gardens.*

OLD BUILDINGS, NEW USES

Colonial optimism of the late 1800s saw grand government buildings replace convict-built structures in the administrative precinct along George Street. The Treasury Building was built in three stages between 1885 and 1928 in elegant, Italian Renaissance style. Across Queen's Park, the less ornate but similar Land Administration Building was completed in 1905. Having outlived their purpose, in the 1990s these buildings were given a new lease of life as a stylish casino and hotel complex.

Top: *Brisbane's Conrad Treasury Casino occupies the gracious building that was formerly the State Treasury Building.*
Above: *(Left) The main casino entrance on Queen Street. (Right) The casino's Elizabeth Street entrance.*

Top: *The William Jolly Bridge connects Grey Street on the south side with Skew Street, and thence Roma Street and the city.*
Above: *The Goodwill Bridge links the South Bank precinct to QUT's Gardens Point campus and the City Botanic Gardens beyond.*

BRISBANE'S BRIDGES

Nine major bridges span the Brisbane River – their distinctive architecture makes each a prominent landmark. The Victoria Toll Bridge, completed in 1874, was the first steel bridge to span the river, but it was swept away in the 1893 floods. The present Victoria Bridge is the third incarnation; a memorial arch at South Bank marks the remains of the second bridge. The Story Bridge, opened in 1940, has a 282-metre span and is the largest steel cantilevered bridge in the country. Downriver at Eagle Farm, the sleek arch of the Gateway Bridge forms part of an eastern city bypass for traffic between the north and south coasts. Opened in 2001, the Goodwill Bridge enables pedestrians and cyclists to cross the river between the South Bank Parklands and Gardens Point.

Top: *The Merivale Rail Bridge seen from the William Jolly Bridge.* **Above:** *The graceful spans of the Victoria Bridge and the Riverside Expressway seen at dusk.*
Below: *(Left) Structural details of the upper part of the Story Bridge. (Right) The Walter Taylor Bridge and its accompanying rail bridge at Indooroopilly.*

UNIQUELY BRISBANE

Brisbanites have fashioned a capital city of unique appearance and atmosphere. It is a people's city where humour and a dash of tropical colour balance day to day business concerns. The cityscape invites public involvement: it has everything from walking trails of heritage buildings to riverfront rock climbs and model dinosaurs that tout museum visits. Through the year the people of Brisbane take to the streets with a full program of festivals and cultural events.

Top: (Left) This elegant building on the corner of Alice and Edward Streets is now a gallery and restaurant. (Right) The Palace Backpackers – budget accommodation with lace. **Above:** Human factor figures from Expo 88, relocated in Ann Street.

Above and clockwise: *A lifesize figure of a Triceratops crouches in a niche on the Grey Street side of the Queensland Museum; a nineteenth-century warehouse on Edward Street; this mosaic, designed by Lindsay Edwards, has decorated the annexe of the old State Library since the late 1950s; abseiling down the cliffs at Kangaroo Point.*

Above: *The hilly western suburbs are notable for their gardens and the "Queenslanders" with their galvanised-iron roofs.*
Opposite: *Typical Queensland houses with details of their timber and wrought-iron trimmings.*

BRISBANE STYLE

Brisbane's signature housing style is known as the "Queenslander". Designed to lessen the effects of cyclones, floods, termites and humid summers, these timber houses sit high above the ground on tin-capped hardwood stumps. Deep verandahs and high-pitched roofs, traditionally red or green, help keep them cool inside. These practical dwellings perch precariously on city ridges to catch prevailing breezes, whimsically embellished with elaborate trimmings of white timber or wrought iron. Proud owners lovingly restore these nineteenth-century houses, while builders of new homes often seek to replicate their charm and grace.

Above: *The main buildings of the St Lucia campus of the University of Queensland are constructed from Helidon sandstone.*
Opposite top: *An aerial view of the St Lucia campus of the University of Queensland.*
Opposite bottom: *Inside the Gardens Point campus of the Queensland University of Technology.*

PLACES OF LEARNING

Students find themselves in some of Brisbane's most delightful settings. The central campus of the Queensland University of Technology lies between the City Botanic Gardens and the South Brisbane Reach of the river. Its research and education programs make the most of this CBD location to foster collaboration with business and industry, while its other parkland campuses are at Kelvin Grove and Carseldine. Although established in 1909, the University of Queensland did not move to its main site at St Lucia until 1948. The Great Court, ringed by handsome sandstone buildings, is the hub of this 110-hectare campus. The University of Queensland also has campuses at Ipswich and Gatton. Further afield, near Mt Gravatt, two Griffith University campuses lie in a peaceful woodland setting bordering Toohey Forest. Griffith also has a Gold Coast campus.

BRISBANE'S WILDLIFE

Close encounters of the wildlife kind are common in Brisbane. Many native animals have adapted to town life: the city's backyards, parks and reserves are home to possums, lizards, frogs and all manner of birds, including intrepid Australian Brush-turkeys, which are more than a match for the cats of Brisbane. Kookaburras, magpies and parrots lead the dawn choruses of feathered songsters, while the chatter of fruit bats and possums' noisy squabbles are familiar night sounds. Woodland-dwelling Koalas are some of Brisbane's more elusive inhabitants, but they, along with other famous Australian animals, can be found at local wildlife sanctuaries.

Top: *(Left) Australian King-Parrots are common in the suburbs. (Right) A Common Brushtail Possum in a Brisbane garden.*
Above: *(Left) Eastern Water Dragons frequent Brisbane's creeks. (Right) Green Tree-frogs flourish in the city's backyards.*
Opposite: *A Koala and ranger at Lone Pine Koala Sanctuary, Fig Tree Pocket, which is accessible by road or river.*

Above: *The heavenly blue-mauve of Jacaranda flowers gives accent to a garden.*

Opposite, top and clockwise: *Brisbane's suburbs become a mosaic of Jacaranda blossom in spring and early summer; Orchard Butterfly; Wanderer Butterfly; the city framed by New Farm Park's Jacaranda trees.*

BRISBANE IN SPRINGTIME

Spring arrives in Brisbane in late August. As native wattles and pea-bushes fade, city parks and suburban gardens come ablaze with the purple hues of Jacaranda trees. Fallen blossoms carpet the ground beneath the Jacaranda's emerging canopy of feathery leaves. Brisbanites have taken this Brazilian native to heart and regard it as the city's unofficial floral emblem.

Springtime's heady mix of perfumes and colours are intensified by flowering Bauhinias, Poinsettias, Flame trees and Silky Oaks. Spring is also the time of the River*festival*. This celebration of Brisbane, its life and its river takes place in September at outdoor venues throughout the city centre.

Above: *State of Origin, the annual rugby league tournament between New South Wales and Queensland, is fiercely contested and passionately supported. Queensland's pride in the maroon jersey is matched only by a spirited contempt for the sky blue.*

THIS SPORTING LIFE

The people of Brisbane are sports mad and indulge their passion in all seasons and all weather. On weekends adults and children take to city sporting venues and coastal beaches for local competitions in everything from hockey and football to surf lifesaving and triathlons.

Brisbanites are avid spectators and the city's landmark stadiums – the Brisbane Cricket Ground at Woolloongabba (the Gabba); Ballymore; QSAC (commonly known by its former name, QEII); and Suncorp Stadium (or Lang Park) – are home grounds for many of Queensland's premier teams. The city's sporting facilities have also played host to exciting international competitions, including the Goodwill Games, the Commonwealth Games and Olympic Games events.

Above: *Cricket is a favourite sport for many Brisbanites.* **Below:** *A Gold Coast Iron Woman competition.*

MORETON BAY

Moreton Bay shelters behind a chain of massive sand islands beginning in the south with South Stradbroke Island and ending in the north at Bribie Island. Numerous smaller islands and sandbanks create a maze of waterways beloved by fishing and boating enthusiasts. Dugong and Bottlenose Dolphins inhabit the bay's protected waters, while migrating Humpback Whales use it as a resting place. Vehicular ferries and water taxis make regular trips to the larger islands, all of which are ideal for family holidays.

The bay's western shoreline was the scene of Brisbane's first settlement, at Redcliffe, and the area later became a seaside retreat for the colonial elite. Attractive suburban enclaves now line the shore and the area is a popular destination for bayside day trips.

Above: *Feeding Bottlenose Dolphins at Moreton Island.*

Top left and clockwise: *Mangroves grow on the shores of Moreton Bay; Frenchman's Beach, North Stradbroke Island; the timber lighthouse at Cleveland Point, built in 1864; dune-surfers set off with their toboggan boards on Moreton Island; ferries carry vehicles and passengers to the islands of Moreton Bay.*

Top: (Left) Sea World, on The Spit, is a popular Gold Coast attraction. (Right) Dreamworld offers all sorts of thrills, including Tiger Island.

Above: The Gold Coast breaks are famous among surfers.

Below: (Left) Feeding the lorikeets at Currumbin Sanctuary. (Right) The gateway to paradise at Surfers Paradise on the Gold Coast.

Above: *An aerial view over Coolangatta on the southern Gold Coast to the hinterland beyond.*

SOUTH TO THE GOLD COAST

The Gold Coast, an hour's drive from Brisbane, is a magic holiday destination. Its sheltered waterways and sun-drenched beaches stretch 50 kilometres south from Sanctuary Cove to Coolangatta. As well as sun, sand and surf, this seaside playground offers the sophistication of international resorts and the excitement of theme-park visits. It is also a shopper's paradise with a staggering array of retail venues that will tempt serious buyers and leisurely browsers alike. Cafés, clubs and restaurants keep the Gold Coast glittering long after sunset.

Above: *Elabana Falls, Lamington National Park.*
Opposite, top left and clockwise: *Chalahn Falls, Lamington National Park; meeting the parrots at O'Reilly's Guesthouse on the Lamington Plateau; Natural Bridge, Springbrook National Park; rainforest, Mt Tamborine; the edge of the Lamington Plateau.*

THE SOUTH-EASTERN FORESTS

A wonderland of dramatic valleys and escarpments lies within the Scenic Rim, a 300-kilometre arc of ranges to the south-east of Brisbane. A series of national parks, including Tamborine and the World Heritage Listed Springbrook and Lamington, showcases some of the world's remaining stands of subtropical rainforest. Wildlife is plentiful and many animals show little fear of humans. It is outstanding bushwalking country with woodland and forest trails that feature panoramic views and mountain creeks tumbling to crystal-clear rockpools.

Beyond the low profile of Bribie Island lies the Sunshine Coast, a favoured destination for vacations and weekend getaways where superb beaches intersected by scenic headlands and estuaries stretch from Caloundra to Noosa Heads. In the undulating hinterland, small farms, charming towns and striking landscapes spread west from the coast to the Conondale and Jimna ranges: this area is known for its galleries, cottage industries, exotic crops and dairy products. The coastline continues its northward sweep from the Noosa River mouth along the Cooloola sand mass to Wide Bay, Tin Can Bay and Fraser Island, which is a World Heritage Area of towering dunes, perched lakes and majestic forests, and is the largest sand island in the world.

Top left and clockwise: *Noosa; Mooloolaba; enthralled crowds flock to Australia Zoo — the brainchild of the late Steve Irwin; Noosa Beach; Maroochydore; Pumicestone Passage separates Bribie from the mainland.*

Above: *The Glass House Mountains are volcanic remnants that rise amongst orchards and farms just north of Brisbane.*
Below: *On Fraser Island, Waddy Point (left), and perched lakes lying in hollows between massive sand dunes (right).*